Quit Smoking
Coloring Journal,
Stop the Smoking Habit
A Journal to Help You
Quit Smoking

By D. Smoot

ISBN-13: 978-1986985642
ISBN-10: 1986985644

Dedication

Dedicate your Journal to the people in your life that you are quitting smoking for, who are helping you quit and/or are quitting with you.

_____

_____

_____

_____

_____

_____

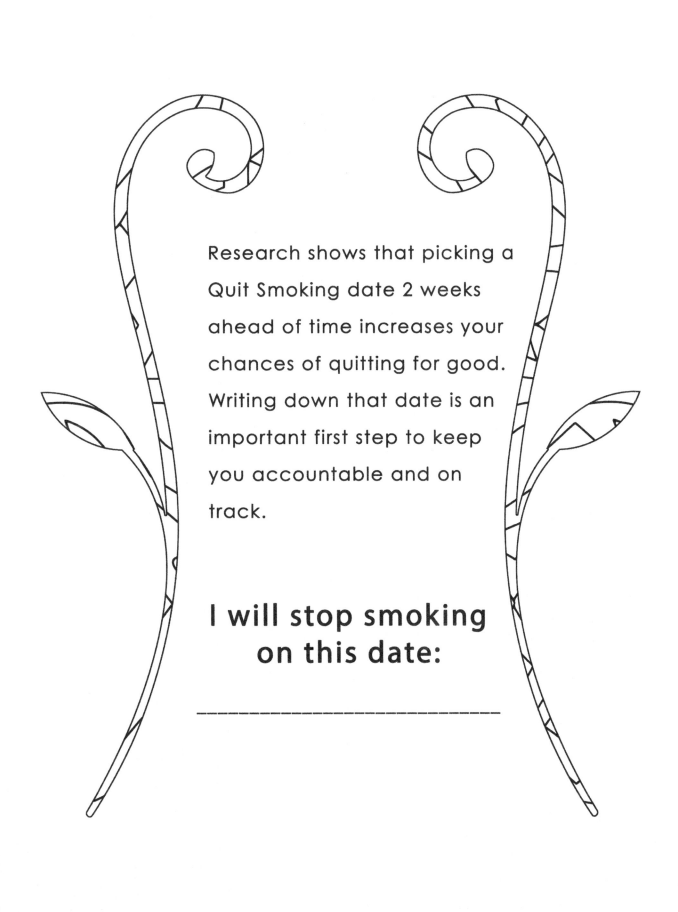

Research shows that picking a Quit Smoking date 2 weeks ahead of time increases your chances of quitting for good. Writing down that date is an important first step to keep you accountable and on track.

I will stop smoking on this date:

_____

5 Steps To Quit For Life

1. Quit at your own pace.
2. Conquer your urges to smoke.
3. Use medications, gum, patches and/or lozenges.
4. Control your environment.
5. Get social support.

Why I Want To Quit Smoking

_____

_____

_____

_____

_____

_____

_____

_____

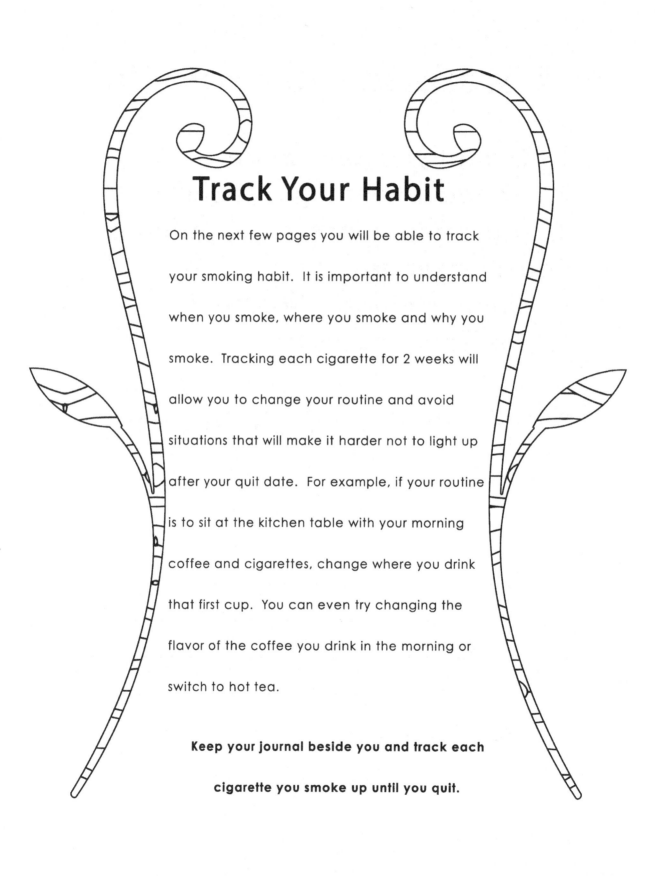

Track Your Habit

On the next few pages you will be able to track your smoking habit. It is important to understand when you smoke, where you smoke and why you smoke. Tracking each cigarette for 2 weeks will allow you to change your routine and avoid situations that will make it harder not to light up after your quit date. For example, if your routine is to sit at the kitchen table with your morning coffee and cigarettes, change where you drink that first cup. You can even try changing the flavor of the coffee you drink in the morning or switch to hot tea.

Keep your journal beside you and track each cigarette you smoke up until you quit.

Track Your Habit

For the next 2 weeks, keep track of every time you smoke, what you are doing, where you are, and how many you smoke at that time.

Time	Activity						Mood						Other Activities, Feelings - Describe	Need Rating		
	Food	Alcohol	Coffee	Friends	Famliy	Driving	Angry	Happy	Sad	Bored	Relaxed	Tired		Low	Medium	High

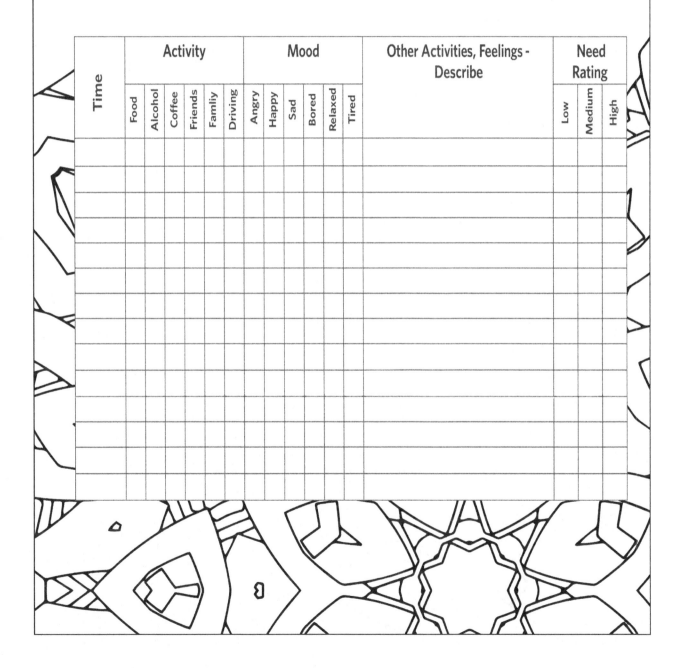

Track Your Habit

Keep track of every time you smoke, what you are doing, where you are, and how many you smoke at that time.

Time	Activity						Mood						Other Activities, Feelings - Describe	Need Rating		
	Food	Alcohol	Coffee	Friends	Famliy	Driving	Angry	Happy	Sad	Bored	Relaxed	Tired		Low	Medium	High

Track Your Habit

Keep track of every time you smoke, what you are doing, where you are, and how many you smoke at that time.

Time	Activity						Mood						Other Activities, Feelings - Describe	Need Rating		
	Food	Alcohol	Coffee	Friends	Famliy	Driving	Angry	Happy	Sad	Bored	Relaxed	Tired		Low	Medium	High

Track Your Habit

Keep track of every time you smoke, what you are doing, where you are, and how many you smoke at that time.

Time	Activity						Mood						Other Activities, Feelings - Describe	Need Rating		
	Food	Alcohol	Coffee	Friends	Famliy	Driving	Angry	Happy	Sad	Bored	Relaxed	Tired		Low	Medium	High

Track Your Habit

Keep track of every time you smoke, what you are doing, where you are, and how many you smoke at that time.

Time	Activity						Mood						Other Activities, Feelings - Describe	Need Rating		
	Food	Alcohol	Coffee	Friends	Famliy	Driving	Angry	Happy	Sad	Bored	Relaxed	Tired		Low	Medium	High

Track Your Habit

Keep track of every time you smoke, what you are doing, where you are, and how many you smoke at that time.

Time	Activity						Mood						Other Activities, Feelings - Describe	Need Rating		
	Food	Alcohol	Coffee	Friends	Famliy	Driving	Angry	Happy	Sad	Bored	Relaxed	Tired		Low	Medium	High

Track Your Habit

Keep track of every time you smoke, what you are doing, where you are, and how many you smoke at that time.

Time	Activity						Mood						Other Activities, Feelings - Describe	Need Rating		
	Food	Alcohol	Coffee	Friends	Famliy	Driving	Angry	Happy	Sad	Bored	Relaxed	Tired		Low	Medium	High

2 Weeks Before Your Quit Date

1. Things you like to do other than smoking._____

_____

_____

_____

_____

_____

2. How will you deal with urges to smoke?_____

_____

_____

_____

_____

3. Become active at least 3 times per week. If you have a

medical issue or haven't been active in awhile, consult a

doctor first.

4. Use your tracker to track each cigarette.

Tips For This Week

- Delay your first cigarette of the day for as long as you can.

- Try to only smoke one per hour.

- Put your cigarettes somewhere that makes you have to get up to get them. For example, in a cabinet, in your car, etc. Don't make it easy to have one lit before you realize it.

- Before you smoke each cigarette, think about why you are smoking at that moment. Did you have a craving, are you on the phone, are your driving? Remember to track each cigarette on your Smoking Tracker.

How Have You Changed Your Smoking Habit This Week?_____

_____

_____

_____

_____

Track Your Habit

Keep track of every time you smoke, what you are doing, where you are, and how many you smoke at that time.

Time	Activity						Mood						Other Activities, Feelings - Describe	Need Rating		
	Food	Alcohol	Coffee	Friends	Famliy	Driving	Angry	Happy	Sad	Bored	Relaxed	Tired		Low	Medium	High

Track Your Habit

Keep track of every time you smoke, what you are doing, where you are, and how many you smoke at that time.

Time	Activity						Mood						Other Activities, Feelings - Describe	Need Rating		
	Food	Alcohol	Coffee	Friends	Famliy	Driving	Angry	Happy	Sad	Bored	Relaxed	Tired		Low	Medium	High

Track Your Habit

Keep track of every time you smoke, what you are doing, where you are, and how many you smoke at that time.

Time	Activity						Mood						Other Activities, Feelings - Describe	Need Rating		
	Food	Alcohol	Coffee	Friends	Famliy	Driving	Angry	Happy	Sad	Bored	Relaxed	Tired		Low	Medium	High

Track Your Habit

Keep track of every time you smoke, what you are doing, where you are, and how many you smoke at that time.

Time	Activity						Mood						Other Activities, Feelings - Describe	Need Rating		
	Food	Alcohol	Coffee	Friends	Famliy	Driving	Angry	Happy	Sad	Bored	Relaxed	Tired		Low	Medium	High

Track Your Habit

Keep track of every time you smoke, what you are doing, where you are, and how many you smoke at that time.

Time	Activity						Mood						Other Activities, Feelings - Describe	Need Rating		
	Food	Alcohol	Coffee	Friends	Famliy	Driving	Angry	Happy	Sad	Bored	Relaxed	Tired		Low	Medium	High

Track Your Habit

Keep track of every time you smoke, what you are doing, where you are, and how many you smoke at that time.

Time	Activity						Mood						Other Activities, Feelings - Describe	Need Rating		
	Food	Alcohol	Coffee	Friends	Famliy	Driving	Angry	Happy	Sad	Bored	Relaxed	Tired		Low	Medium	High

Track Your Habit

Keep track of every time you smoke, what you are doing, where you are, and how many you smoke at that time.

Time	Activity						Mood						Other Activities, Feelings - Describe	Need Rating		
	Food	Alcohol	Coffee	Friends	Famliy	Driving	Angry	Happy	Sad	Bored	Relaxed	Tired		Low	Medium	High

1 Week Before Your Quit Date

1. Stop smoking in your car and home

2. Practice quitting for a few hours at a time. These are called "mini quits" and are useful to allow you to start coping with the urges to smoke

3. If your doctor has prescribed medication, start taking it this week so it will be built up in your system on quit day.

4. Start gathering your supplies such as nicotine gum, lozenges, patches, water, straws or stir sticks. Pick up healthy snacks such as celery, carrots, nuts or anything that will keep your hands and mouth busy. Stay away from candy and sweets so you won't gain weight and lose your desire to quit.

5. Take up a hobby that keeps your hands busy while you watch television or for when you are bored. Try coloring, quilting, sewing, drawing or puzzles. These things will also keep your mind busy so you won't think about smoking.

Tips For This Week

- This week you should start finding ways to change your daily routine. Get up later so you don't have time to smoke, drink tea instead of coffee, etc.
- Get adult coloring books, puzzle books, or a new book to read so you have things to do. Boredom is a huge smoking trigger.
- Join a support group on Facebook, Twitter or in your home town. It can be helpful to talk to others who know what you are going through and will not judge you.
- Keep remembering to track each cigarette on your Smoking Tracker.

What did you do this week to prepare for your quit date?_____

_____

_____

_____

_____

_____

The Day Before Your Quit Date

1. Vacuum out your car and get a car air freshener. Wash the ashtray in your car. Fill it with sunflower seeds or flowers.

2. Review the instructions for your nicotine replacement therapy. Make sure you know the right way to use them and have plenty on hand so you don't run out in this critical first smoke free week.

3. Decide how you will manage stress. Try deep breathing, meditation, yoga or coloring.

4. Wash your bed linens, curtains, and anything else in your home that smells like smoke. Clean up any ashes.

5. Before you go to bed, throw away all lighters and cigarettes. Wash all ashtrays and put them away or throw them out.

Tips For Today

- It will be easier to quit smoking if you wake up tomorrow and don't smoke, rather than quitting in the middle of the day. This will allow you to sleep through the worst cravings as the nicotine leaves your body.

- Start brushing your teeth right after eating. This gets you away from the table and gives you something else to focus on.

  Look over your smoking tracker so you can be prepared for your smoking triggers.

- Make a list of rewards for staying smoke free for 1 week, 1 month and 1 year. Use the money you are saving from not smoking to pay for your rewards.

1 Week Reward _____

1 Month Reward _____

1 Year Reward _____

Your First Day Smoke Free...

Congratulations on waking up a non-smoker today!

You will be surprised at how easy today will be.
The most important thing to remember today is you have prepared for this. You have all of your supplies and you know how to beat your urges to smoke when your triggers pop up. Make sure you get out of bed quickly and attack the day!

While you will think a lot about cigarettes today, you can smile knowing that they do not have a hold over you anymore.

When the craving tries to overcome you, just think, you have already went hours without a cigarette and if you decide to have just one more, that cigarette will only help your craving for an hour or so and then you will want another one. "Just one more" is not worth erasing all the time you have went without one.

Use your nicotine replacement and/or do an activity that makes smoking impossible. It will get easier.
You can do this!

Nicotine Withdrawal Symptoms:

Urge to Smoke	Increased Appetite
Anxiety	Restlessness
Depressed Mood	Difficulty Concentrating
Irritability	Frustration
Insomnia	Anger

Speak with your doctor if any of the symptoms become severe. Also, be aware of any side effects of prescribed medications.

1. What helped you the most to beat the urges to smoke today?

_____

_____

_____

_____

2. What helped the least or not at all?

_____

_____

_____

_____

3. When did you have the worst urges to smoke?_____

_____

_____

4. Which withdrawal symptoms did you notice?_____

_____

_____

5. How do you feel at the end of the day?_____

_____

_____

_____

DATE: _____

24 HOURS AFTER QUITTING YOUR BLOOD PRESSURE AND PULSE MAY DROP.

1. Did you have more or less urges to smoke today?_____

_____

_____

2. How did you get through your cravings to smoke?_____

_____

_____

_____

3. How do you feel today?_____

_____

_____

_____

_____

_____

_____

_____

_____

_____

_____

DATE: _____

48 HOURS after quitting your nerve endings start to regrow and your ability to smell & taste will improve.

1. Did you have more or less urges to smoke today?_____

_____

_____

2. How did you get through your cravings to smoke?_____

_____

_____

_____

3. How do you feel today?_____

_____

_____

_____

_____

_____

_____

_____

_____

‐‐

‐‐

‐‐

‐‐

‐‐

‐‐

‐‐

DATE: _____

3 DAYS after quitting your symptoms of chemical withdrawal are beginning to decrease.

1. Did you have more or less urges to smoke today?_____

_____

_____

2. How did you get through your cravings to smoke?_____

_____

_____

_____

3. How do you feel today?_____

_____

_____

_____

_____

_____

_____

_____

_____

_____

_____

_____

_____

_____

_____

_____

_____

DATE: _____

4 DAYS after quitting your breathing is becoming easier as your lung functions are beginning to improve.

1. Did you have more or less urges to smoke today?_____

_____

_____

2. How did you get through your cravings to smoke?_____

_____

_____

_____

3. How do you feel today?_____

_____

_____

_____

_____

_____

_____

_____

_____

_____

_____

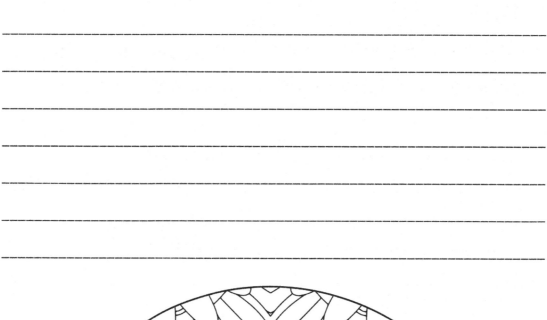

DATE: _____

Today is a good day to steam clean your carpets &
furniture to remove the smell and residue left from
the cigarettes.

1. Did you have more or less urges to smoke today?_____

_____

_____

2. How did you get through your cravings to smoke?_____

_____

_____

_____

3. How do you feel today?_____

_____

_____

_____

_____

_____

_____

_____

_____

_____

_____

_____

_____

_____

_____

_____

_____

_____

DATE: _____

You may cough more after you quit smoking. This is the lungs clearing themselves. The coughing will decrease over the next 9 months.

1. Did you have more or less urges to smoke today?_____

_____

_____

2. How did you get through your cravings to smoke?_____

_____

_____

_____

3. How do you feel today?_____

_____

_____

_____

_____

_____

_____

_____

_____

_____

_____

DATE: _____

CONGRATULATIONS! You have been smoke free for 1 week! Reward yourself with something special today from the money you have saved.

1. Did you have more or less urges to smoke today?_____

_____

_____

2. How did you get through your cravings to smoke?_____

_____

_____

_____

3. How do you feel today?_____

_____

_____

_____

_____

_____

_____

_____

_____

_____

_____

DATE: _____

Water will speed up the nicotine detox & will help ease your cough by making it easier for your lungs to clear the mucus. Start drinking 8 glasses per day.

Water Tracker ⬥⬥⬥⬥⬥⬥⬥⬥

1. Did you have more or less urges to smoke today?_____

_____

_____

2. How did you get through your cravings to smoke?_____

_____

_____

_____

3. How do you feel today?_____

_____

_____

_____

_____

_____

_____

_____

DATE: _____

Vigorous exercise can provide the dopamine release you used to get from cigarettes. Staying active will also speed up your body's repair process.

Water Tracker ⬦⬦⬦⬦⬦⬦⬦

1. Did you have more or less urges to smoke today?_____

_____

_____

2. How did you get through your cravings to smoke?_____

_____

_____

_____

3. How do you feel today?_____

_____

_____

_____

_____

_____

_____

_____

DATE: _____

Find some new recipes to try.

Cooking will take advantage of your improved

sense of smell and taste.

Water Tracker ⬦⬦⬦⬦⬦⬦⬦⬦

1. Did you have more or less urges to smoke today?_____

_____

_____

2. How did you get through your cravings to smoke?_____

_____

_____

_____

3. How do you feel today?_____

_____

_____

_____

_____

_____

_____

_____

DATE: _____

Deep breathing will fight cravings since it relaxes you. The extra oxygen will also help headaches and release the rest of the residual nicotine in your lungs.

Water Tracker ⬭⬭⬭⬭⬭⬭⬭⬭

1. Did you have more or less urges to smoke today?_____

_____

_____

2. How did you get through your cravings to smoke?_____

_____

_____

_____

3. How do you feel today?_____

_____

_____

_____

_____

_____

_____

_____

_____

_____

_____

_____

_____

_____

_____

DATE: _____

It's important to find new ways to relax and calm yourself without nicotine. Buy a stress relief ball, silly putty, etc, to begin new healthy stress relief habits.

Water Tracker ○○○○○○○○

1. Did you have more or less urges to smoke today?_____

_____

_____

2. How did you get through your cravings to smoke?_____

_____

_____

_____

3. How do you feel today?_____

_____

_____

_____

_____

_____

_____

_____

_____

DATE: _____

Nicotine suppresses the effects of caffeine. As you stop using nicotine replacements, coffee and soda will have a stronger effect on your body & heart.

Water Tracker ○○○○○○○○

1. Did you have more or less urges to smoke today?_____

_____

_____

2. How did you get through your cravings to smoke?_____

_____

_____

_____

3. How do you feel today?_____

_____

_____

_____

_____

_____

_____

_____

DATE: _____

The yellow stains on your teeth & fingers will start to fade. Your lips will start looking better as you are less likely to have burns or mouth sores.

Water Tracker ◇◇◇◇◇◇◇◇

1. Did you have more or less urges to smoke today?_____

_____

_____

2. How did you get through your cravings to smoke?_____

_____

_____

_____

3. How do you feel today?_____

_____

_____

_____

_____

_____

_____

_____

_____

DATE: _____

2-4 Weeks after quitting the psychological effects of withdrawal will stop. You should not have any nicotine withdrawal symptoms after 4 weeks.

Water Tracker ⬠⬠⬠⬠⬠⬠⬠⬠

1. Did you have more or less urges to smoke today?_____

_____

_____

2. How did you get through your cravings to smoke?_____

_____

_____

_____

3. How do you feel today?_____

_____

_____

_____

_____

_____

_____

_____

_____

DATE: _____

It's all about choices! You choose and you make the rules, not the tobacco companies and not nicotine addiction.

Water Tracker ⬭⬭⬭⬭⬭⬭⬭⬭

1. Did you have more or less urges to smoke today?_____

_____

_____

2. How did you get through your cravings to smoke?_____

_____

_____

_____

3. How do you feel today?_____

_____

_____

_____

_____

_____

_____

_____

_____

_____

_____

_____

_____

_____

DATE: _____

Most people who have quit smoking have had at least one unsuccessful try. It's not important how many times you try, just that you eventually quit.

Water Tracker   ○○○○○○○○

1. Did you have more or less urges to smoke today?_____

_____

_____

2. How did you get through your cravings to smoke?_____

_____

_____

_____

3. How do you feel today?_____

_____

_____

_____

_____

_____

_____

_____

_____

_____

_____

_____

_____

_____

_____

_____

DATE: _____

Quitting smoking is a marathon, not a sprint. It is not a one time attempt, but a continual effort over a long period of time.

Water Tracker ○○○○○○○○

1. Did you have more or less urges to smoke today?_____

_____

_____

2. How did you get through your cravings to smoke?_____

_____

_____

_____

3. How do you feel today?_____

_____

_____

_____

_____

_____

_____

_____

_____

DATE: _____

Every beginning is difficult, but it does get easier as time goes by.

Water Tracker ⬭⬭⬭⬭⬭⬭⬭⬭

1. Did you have more or less urges to smoke today?_____

_____

_____

2. How did you get through your cravings to smoke?_____

_____

_____

_____

3. How do you feel today?_____

_____

_____

_____

_____

_____

_____

_____

_____

DATE: _____

Today is a good day to remember all the reasons why you wanted to quit smoking in the first place to stay motivated.

Water Tracker ◊◊◊◊◊◊◊◊

1. Did you have more or less urges to smoke today?_____

_____

_____

2. How did you get through your cravings to smoke?_____

_____

_____

_____

3. How do you feel today?_____

_____

_____

_____

_____

_____

_____

_____

_____

DATE: _____

Believing in yourself is the first step to success.

You are as strong as you think you are.

Your strength is all in your head.

Water Tracker ⬠⬠⬠⬠⬠⬠⬠⬠

1. Did you have more or less urges to smoke today?_____

_____

_____

2. How did you get through your cravings to smoke?_____

_____

_____

_____

3. How do you feel today?_____

_____

_____

_____

_____

_____

_____

_____

_____

DATE: _____

Self-awareness, conscience, independent will, and creative imagination...these give us the ultimate human freedom, the power to choose and change.

Water Tracker ⬭⬭⬭⬭⬭⬭⬭⬭

1. Did you have more or less urges to smoke today?_____

_____

_____

2. How did you get through your cravings to smoke?_____

_____

_____

_____

3. How do you feel today?_____

_____

_____

_____

_____

_____

_____

_____

DATE: _____

Quitting smoking is a good test of one's character.
Pass this test and you accomplish so much more
than getting rid of one bad habit.

Water Tracker ⬭⬭⬭⬭⬭⬭⬭⬭

1. Did you have more or less urges to smoke today?_____

_____

_____

2. How did you get through your cravings to smoke?_____

_____

_____

_____

3. How do you feel today?_____

_____

_____

_____

_____

_____

_____

_____

_____

DATE: _____

The choices you make today have a huge impact on your future. Choosing to remain smoke free will impact your future health and happiness.

Water Tracker ⭘⭘⭘⭘⭘⭘⭘⭘

1. Did you have more or less urges to smoke today?_____

_____

_____

2. How did you get through your cravings to smoke?_____

_____

_____

_____

3. How do you feel today?_____

_____

_____

_____

_____

_____

_____

_____

_____

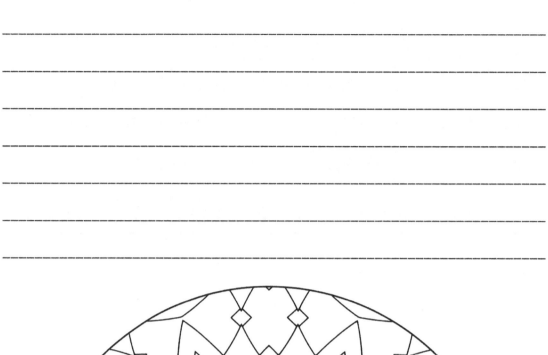

DATE: _____

The process of quitting smoking doesn't end with the last cigarette. Victory belongs to those who can remain smoke free.

Water Tracker ⬡⬡⬡⬡⬡⬡⬡⬡

1. Did you have more or less urges to smoke today?_____

_____

_____

2. How did you get through your cravings to smoke?_____

_____

_____

_____

3. How do you feel today?_____

_____

_____

_____

_____

_____

_____

_____

_____

DATE: _____

Who we are is a result of what we have chosen to do. Never forget that you have chosen to be a non-smoker, no one forced it on you.

Water Tracker ⬡⬡⬡⬡⬡⬡⬡⬡

1. Did you have more or less urges to smoke today?_____

_____

_____

2. How did you get through your cravings to smoke?_____

_____

_____

_____

3. How do you feel today?_____

_____

_____

_____

_____

_____

_____

_____

_____

DATE: _____

Always think, walk, talk and act like a non-smoker
and you will be one for the rest of your life.

Water Tracker ◌◌◌◌◌◌◌◌

1. Did you have more or less urges to smoke today?_____

_____

_____

2. How did you get through your cravings to smoke?_____

_____

_____

_____

3. How do you feel today?_____

_____

_____

_____

_____

_____

_____

_____

_____

DATE: _____

Always think, walk, talk and act like a non-smoker
and you will be one for the rest of your life.

Water Tracker ⬡⬡⬡⬡⬡⬡⬡⬡

1. Did you have more or less urges to smoke today?_____

_____

_____

2. How did you get through your cravings to smoke?_____

_____

_____

_____

3. How do you feel today?_____

_____

_____

_____

_____

_____

_____

_____

_____

DATE: _____

You can lie to and hide your actions from others, but you can never fool yourself about what you have done. You must quit for yourself first.

Water Tracker ОООООООО

1. Did you have more or less urges to smoke today?_____

_____

_____

2. How did you get through your cravings to smoke?_____

_____

_____

_____

3. How do you feel today?_____

_____

_____

_____

_____

_____

_____

_____

DATE: _____

Tomorrow it will be 30 days since your quit date.
Take a moment to write about how you feel, both
physically and mentally.

Water Tracker   ○○○○○○○○

DATE: _____

CONGRATULATIONS! It has been 30 days since your

quit date. You are on the road to remaining smoke

free. How will you reward yourself?

_____

_____

_____

_____

_____

_____

How has quitting smoking changed your life?_____

_____

_____

_____

_____

_____

_____

_____

Water Tracker   ○○○○○○○○

CHECK OFF THE BENEFITS YOU FEEL AND
ENJOY NOW THAT YOU ARE SMOKE FREE:

- ☐ I can breathe better
- ☐ I have an improved sense of smell
- ☐ I smell better
- ☐ My food tastes better
- ☐ I don't cough anymore
- ☐ I don't have trouble breathing
- ☐ I have more energy
- ☐ I feel more in control of my life
- ☐ I feel a sense of freedom
- ☐ I have saved money
- ☐ My house is cleaner
- ☐ I feel good about myself
- ☐ I sleep better
- Add your own:
- ☐
- ☐
- ☐

Of all the benefits, which one is your
favorite, and why?_____

_____

_____

_____

_____

DATE: _____

Keep writing in a journal for as long as it helps you stay a non-smoker. Included are a few lined pages for you to use until you get another one.

Water Tracker ⬡⬡⬡⬡⬡⬡⬡⬡

DATE: _____

Water Tracker   ◇◇◇◇◇◇◇◇

DATE: _____

Water Tracker ◇◇◇◇◇◇◇◇

DATE: _____

Water Tracker ⬦⬦⬦⬦⬦⬦⬦⬦

DATE: _____

Water Tracker ⬦⬦⬦⬦⬦⬦⬦⬦

DATE: _____

Water Tracker ◌◌◌◌◌◌◌◌

DATE: _____

Water Tracker ⬭⬭⬭⬭⬭⬭⬭⬭

DATE: _____

Water Tracker ◊◊◊◊◊◊◊◊

DATE: _____

Water Tracker   ○○○○○○○○

DATE: _____

Water Tracker   ⬯ ⬯ ⬯ ⬯ ⬯ ⬯ ⬯

DATE: _____

Water Tracker   ⬡⬡⬡⬡⬡⬡⬡

DATE: _____

Water Tracker ○○○○○○○○

DATE: _____

Water Tracker   ◊◊◊◊◊◊◊◊

DATE: _____

Water Tracker ⬯⬯⬯⬯⬯⬯⬯⬯

DATE: _____

Water Tracker ⬭⬭⬭⬭⬭⬭⬭

DATE: _____

Water Tracker ⬭⬭⬭⬭⬭⬭⬭

DATE: _____

Water Tracker ◌◌◌◌◌◌◌◌

_____
_____
_____
_____
_____
_____
_____
_____
_____
_____
_____
_____
_____
_____
_____
_____
_____

Track Your Habit

Keep track of every time you smoke, what you are doing, where you are, and how many you smoke at that time.

Time	Activity						Mood						Other Activities, Feelings - Describe	Need Rating		
	Food	Alcohol	Coffee	Friends	Famliy	Driving	Angry	Happy	Sad	Bored	Relaxed	Tired		Low	Medium	High

Track Your Habit

Keep track of every time you smoke, what you are doing, where you are, and how many you smoke at that time.

Time	Activity						Mood						Other Activities, Feelings - Describe	Need Rating		
	Food	Alcohol	Coffee	Friends	Famliy	Driving	Angry	Happy	Sad	Bored	Relaxed	Tired		Low	Medium	High

Made in the USA
Las Vegas, NV
04 November 2021

33695827R00063